HAL•LEONARD
INSTRUMENTAL
PLAY-ALONG

CLARINET

GREAT MOVIE THEMES

CONTENTS

2	Batman Theme	BATMAN
3	Gabriel's Oboe	THE MISSION
4	The Godfather (Love Theme)	THE GODFATHER
6	Gonna Fly Now	ROCKY
8	He's a Pirate	PIRATES OF THE CARIBBEAN
5	Last of the Mohicans (Main Theme)	LAST OF THE MOHICANS
10	Mrs. Darcy	PRIDE AND PREJUDICE
12	My Heart Will Go On (Love Theme from 'Titanic')	TITANIC
13	Now We Are Free	GLADIATOR
14	Over the Rainbow	THE WIZARD OF OZ
15	The Pink Panther	THE PINK PANTHER
16	Star Wars® (Main Theme)	STAR WARS®

To access audio visit:
www.halleonard.com/mylibrary

Enter Code
6080-1231-1510-4981

T0056036

Audio Arrangements by Peter Deneff

ISBN 978-1-4950-0554-1

HAL•LEONARD®
CORPORATION
7777 W. BLUEMOUND RD. P.O. BOX 13819 MILWAUKEE, WI 53213

BATMAN THEME

CLARINET

Music by
NEAL HEFTI

GABRIEL'S OBOE

from the Motion Picture THE MISSION

CLARINET

Music by
ENNIO MORRICONE

THE GODFATHER

(Love Theme)

from the Paramount Picture THE GODFATHER

CLARINET

By NINO ROTA

LAST OF THE MOHICANS

(Main Theme)

from the Twentieth Century Fox Motion Picture THE LAST OF THE MOHICANS

CLARINET

By TREVOR JONES

GONNA FLY NOW

Theme from ROCKY

CLARINET

Words by CAROL CONNORS and AYN ROBBINS
Music by BILL CONTI

mf
f

HE'S A PIRATE

from Walt Disney Pictures' PIRATES OF THE CARIBBEAN:
THE CURSE OF THE BLACK PEARL

CLARINET

Music by
KLAUS BADELT

5

MRS. DARCY

from PRIDE AND PREJUDICE

CLARINET

By DARIO MARIANELLI

mp
mf
Tempo I
mp
2
rit.
More slowly
p
pp

MY HEART WILL GO ON

(Love Theme from 'TITANIC')

from the Paramount and Twentieth Century Fox Motion Picture TITANIC

CLARINET

Music by JAMES HORNER
Lyric by WILL JENNINGS

Slowly, with feeling

NOW WE ARE FREE

from the Dreamworks film GLADIATOR

CLARINET

Written by HANS ZIMMER,
LISA GERRARD and KLAUS BADELT

OVER THE RAINBOW

from THE WIZARD OF OZ

CLARINET

Music by HAROLD ARLEN
Lyric by E.Y. "Yip" HARBURG

THE PINK PANTHER

from THE PINK PANTHER

CLARINET

By HENRY MANCINI

STAR WARS

(Main Theme)

from STAR WARS, THE EMPIRE STRIKES BACK and RETURN OF THE JEDI

CLARINET

Music by
JOHN WILLIAMS